Substance in Shadow

TREENA J. KERR

Substance in Shadow

ISBN 0-9765382-0-2

Cover art 'Danae and the Brazen Tower' by Sir Edward Coley
Bourne-Jones, used with permission of the Ashmolean Museum of
Art and Archeology, Oxford, England.

Printed in USA

Emotionally moving, spiritually uplifting, *Substance in Shadow* wrestles with the burdens and celebrates the joy of living and loving in the shadow of Treena Kerr's two beloveds, her husband Graham and her savior Jesus Christ. Imbued with the wisdom of experience, this book is a personal record of Treena's growth of faith in her creative self and a testament to her faith in God. Whether she is writing laments in the tradition of the Song of Songs or confessing the dark night of her soul during her pilgrim's progress, Treena Kerr emerges whole into the light, full of wonder for this life and hope for the next.

Born in England, Treena married Graham Kerr, moving with the "Galloping Gourmet" to New Zealand then to Canada, living the high life of a celebrity and suffering life-threatening illness before settling into a modest and health-conscious lifestyle in Washington State. An Emmy nominated producer of her husband's television shows, including *Graham Kerr's Gathering Place;* she has been active in the theatre and shown a life-long commitment to her family and friends. Treena is an internationally renowned public speaker who draws from the deep well of her experience for her inspirational message.

Contents

Gratitude

To my Lord Jesus! My husband of 50 years, Graham, who is my best friend! My beloved children Tessa, Andrew and Kareena, and their loves Scott, Janet and Michael. My gift of grandchildren, Matthew, Molly, Brooke, Katherine, Jessica and Sydney. Wendy, our beloved secretary and her family. All my dearest friends, no one could be as blessed, each one a treasure of love. You know who you are. My ever friends!

Introduction

here's music from my soul,
with harmony words, not notes.
internal views, some fragile.
emotion laid dormant in my heart
until actions framed
those hidden thoughts,
with images in words.
mysteries revealed,
creations awesome beauty,
human suffering and sorrow
or the hope of those ideals.
the one who speaks herewith
does merely try to paint
with verse, a whim, a sigh,
a whispered heart's complaint-
albeit sonnet, verse,
new prose or simple art.
so, thus dear friend,
(if I may call you such.)
i pray, a hurt will heal,
a heart forgive and feel
His simple touch this day

A mother's mother

To see her hold,
Watch her nurse,
Her tiny sigh of life.
Witness her love,
Discern her growth,
From child into a wife;
To perceive the peace,
The utter joy;
That beats inside another.
To watch maternal feelings leap
Inside my daughter-mother.
There is a wondrous pain
Of love and awe
Flowing through
This mother's mother.

Glimmer of Wisdom

Silently, the mist of Winter's night
Swirling, twirling around lamps light,
Making halos as through veils of Grace.
Small drops of Creations tears cling
To naked trees with ghostly limps.
Pavements gleam with ebony pools,
Bewitching all with Creations jewels.
Oh silent street, miraculous night,
What are you saying, sight so bright?
I too can have Peace and Outward Light
Inside my heart and soul tonight?

The Meaning of Life

(Before)
What is life?
I turned to look and found that life was – what?
A path on which I wandered, back and forth?
Where was life?
When would I begin to see the reason why?
Were my "doings" right or wrong? Or –
Were they right for me, but wrong for others?
Were others the reason for this life, or me?

Life seemed to leave me drifting
In a bubble without light.
No blues or greens, shades of red
Just opaque nothing – fish-eye dead.

I called, "Life – where are you?
What are you? Who are you?
Can you make my life worthwhile –
So I may make a life of worth for others"

(much later . . .)
Life – I knew not, where, what,
Or who you were.
I searched and searched and searched –
Until one day, a stranger said to me,
"The Man of Life, once said,
'I am the Way,
The Truth
The Life.' "

I knew at last, at last I knew
That Jesus was the Life –
He laid down His life –
That I might lay down mine – for you!

to love as one

to be aware
and love in faith
is all one should desire
to try,
and learn,
and rectify,
some seeming wrong,
this should be done.
yet, do not be alone,
for when two love
one is half
if left,
or leaves
the arms of one
whose life is stressed.
I prefer, to be complete
and walk with you,
along the street
toward the other half of self.
to learn with you
to help,
to understand,
the way we lost ourselves.
we have the right,
to right the wrongs
to each we've made.
no one, alone is wrong,
no one, alone is right;
in marriage, we are one,
and love is ours – not flight!

December 17th 1974

I went to Bethlehem to find
A solace for my tortured mind.
With trepidation as a child,
I lingered with bewildered mind.
A pastor tall and dark did walk
To greet me with a loving smile –
"My name is Pastor Friend," he said
And prayed for my unwary soul,
He said "The angels will rejoice
with Christ and me this very night."

As the congregation prayed
I fell, surprised, upon my knees –
then, wrenched from deep within my shame
a cry of hope was born within my soul,
"Forgive me Jesus," cried my heart,
Repentant tears of sorrow, filled my eyes,
Burning tears began to fall
Then turned into a water fall.

Friends, Ruthie and Michelle,
and daughter Tessa too –
Watched and waited silently.
I stepped – dressed in Ruthie's gown of white
into the concrete bath of blue
filled with ice cold water too –

Thus, baptized, cleansed from sins.
Although I didn't realize how or why –
A course was set to now live by.
The pastor, Chester Friend, did ask,
"How would you like to tarry"?
"What's that" I asked
"Just waiting on the Holy Ghost."
"Well might as well as I am here.
What do I have to do?" I asked
"just kneel and thank our Jesus Christ
for the gift, He wants to give to you."

So there I knelt with eyes tight shut
Saying "thank you" to the name
I had cursed and sworn just hours before.
Suddenly upon closed eyes
A strong light shone. A blinding light.
I opened up my eyes and saw
A Man of brilliance standing there,
a joyous smile upon His face.
There upon my heart, He placed
His gentle Hand; instantly, I was filled,
with knowledge from within
I had His Joy, His Peace and Holy Grace.
and from "my living hell,"
Hope took its place.

God Breathed

The beginning
merely void;
before was naught –
after, was all.
God breathed;
created light
for velvet night
and perfect day.
Cold winds blew,
then ebbed away.
Before was gloom –
after – was gold.
Life began; God Breathed
then came man.
From rib, woman.
God foretold
that all who wait,
for those that will,
shall be complete
from then – until.
But they did eat,
Now we wait
'till all's complete,
we wait. Until?

Ruth

she smiled at me,
i knew she knew.
innocently she did stand
stretching out
her small black hand.
she arrived and shone
with knowledge glowing
from large brown eyes
without music did she sing.
angels must have sang her praise
for her precious faith's bouquet
were the silent prayers,
she prayed for me.

the past

pain is done!
hurts are gone.
no more nagging doubts.
forgiveness bounds
in every step
of this new child in Christ –
because, the gentle touch
of He who suffered
and knew pain,
has wiped away for ever more
old memory's migraine.
no scars to show,
no ugliness
or tortures
from the past.
He took a life
and mended it
making a brand new wife!

Escape

No more people
Sapping energy
No inconsequential
Babble, Blather, talk
Tiring ears and mind.
Like a continuing tuning fork.
No more obligations
To either care or cheer.
No more murmuring sound
Of sympathy insincere.
Just solitude and peace abound
without demands to turn a page,
or stresses to engage.

Yet . . .

Unto an isolated soul
There is an emptiness inside
Which people used to satisfy
With idle chat, sometimes,
lovingly, identifying.
By escaping people
one's Spirit suffers loss,
isolation's lethal.
Despair soon takes its place.

Solitude I know full well is freeing
A time alone with Grace
Much needed in ones life
giving benefit from strife,
After one has been refreshed
by peace and quiet respite
Then one can be blessed
Encouraging with care
Strangers, loved ones, friends.
Tenderness is needed
All persons are unique.

Vanity in Vacuum

people, people, people,
people everywhere.
people talk in circles,
sometimes in a square.
chatter, chatter, chatter, chatter,
chatter causing crime.
chatter people, people chatter,
tongues in overtime.
minds seem blank with idle chatter,
eyelids rarely blink.
people, people, chatter, chatter,
too engrossed to think!
people chatter, chatter people
chattering life away;
futile chatter, barren people,
wasting every day.

Wrinkle in time

At thirty years, one appears.
Discretely and silently
But not quite – invisibly.

At forty, moisturizers, creams,
Lotions, facial aids embrace
This age announcing face.

At fifty, thoughts of face lifts,
Exercise and facials,
Sunscreens, sun hats and bifocals.

At sixty, THE wrinkle,
Has now multiplied it seems,
Taking wrinkles to extremes.

Crinkled lips, once were soft,
Inviting, plump and moist.
We can not in all truth rejoice.

Furrowed alabaster brows,
Crows feet frame sparkling eyes.
The dimples? They are no surprise.

Beloveds, each and every crinkle,
Give character, in every wrinkle
But . . . those brown spots?

A Time to Pray?

The heart beats
In rhythm with one's musings –
Thoughts tumble
A cacophony of words.
Sleep is shallow
Introspection tiles, cascades.
Slumber's oblivion
Is not to be this night.

Enable me

Enable me,
this is my prayer.
I'm in trouble.
Have I lost You?
I can't find You
anywhere!
Enable me,
to know You're near,
close by my side.
You foretold
You'd not forsake me.
Yet, where are You?
Enable me,
I'm afraid;
I've lost myself,
and You have left.
I know you say
that I must trust
and understand
also, have faith
and so believe
that You will never
leave my side, so...
Enable me,
to have no doubts.
Enable me,
to just accept;
You will not stop
Your love for me.
Though, I cannot
at this moment
feel Your Presence
close beside.
Enable me –
to embrace,
not abdicate
my right,
to fight
and win this Holy race.
Amen.

I Am?

<u>What</u> am I?
<u>Who</u> am I?
<u>How</u> am I?

I am Yours!
<u>Your</u> Creation!
Am I as
You wanted me?

Who am I?
I am me.
By Your Grace.
Yes! I am me.

Teach me Your Will
You are my God.
Let Your Spirit
Guide my soul.

I know a Place

I know a place of peace
Where Arbutus trees line the shore
Where Kingfishers sing their evening song,
Cormorants and blue herons call.

I know a place of peace
Beneath cormorants Madrona tree
Where sailboats anchor at eventide
And weary souls seem set free.

I know a place of peace
Where the Lord whispers low
Where eyes can see and ears can hear
When those in prayer commune below.

I know a place of peace
Where Spirits are revitalized
From all earths jaded ways
The hassle, stress of lives.

I know a place of peace
deep within the heart
One simply needs to take the time
To be with Him apart.

I Wonder Why

I wonder why my thoughts rush forth
Speaking words which I regret?
Why do I cuss within my head
When I long pure thoughts instead?

What is it all about, this self called me
Which does wrong while desiring right?
A tongue untamed, one cannot flee,
Clacking like those geese in flight.

I wonder why? I truly try
To make my speech proclaim
With sweet words that stroke the ear
And won't defile His Name.

Yet this untamed tongue of mine
Will run its uninhibited view
You see, without You Lord, I find
There's nothing I can do.

In The Valley

Lord, I'm in the Valley,
Deep within the meads
Where I'll pick the flowers
Replacing them with seeds.
When I've nothing else to do
I'll rest in Valley's shade,
I know not where the path lies
By many tears 'tis veiled.
I do not want to be here
Because I long to see
The peaks of sunny Zion
From the path hidden from me.
I'm down here in the valley;
To rest, I need Your Grace.
With Your Smile upon me
And Your Glory on my face.
Help me Lord to rest here,
Quietly from life's race.
When you choose to show me,
The path to Zion's Place.
I will not fight against Your Will,
You know so well my prayer.
But the waiting is not easy
Lord, help me to prepare.

Seldom

We have two eyes that seldom see,
Two ears that seldom heed
A nose that seldom will delight,
In flowers or a tree.

We only see the outward sign
And seldom look within
We seldom seek a new idea
Thus never can begin.

We seldom listen properly
We seldom have the mind
To listen to another's cries
Or give them of our time.

Self-worth

I wandered lonely through the fields
whilst searching for a worth in self.
I saw fresh leaves upon old trees;
wild flowers dressing fields anew
brought butterflies of every hue,
each uniquely individual.
The smallest wing, the tiniest petal
each so delicately settled.
Perfection – Worth a lingering stare.
Nature's self-worth was everywhere.

I stirred upon the rugged fence
on which I sat and there did muse,
"I too am fashioned by the Hand
that has created nature's way!"
Suddenly – a restless breeze breathed
a solace prayer into my heart.

"The secret of mankind's self-worth
is through the searching soul's rebirth.
Believe and trust in Me, my Child,
My inward care will soon disclose –
all of Creation is divine;
though nature's breathless beauty blinds,
nothing compares with "humankind!"

With heart and soul restored in Him,
escorted by the Comforter –
I returned, fixed in Love and hope,
to wander lonely never more –
for now, I knew His original intent,
was to be His humble instrument
that lays close by His feet to use
for those that need Him introduced.

So Be It

He came.
He saw.
He overcame.
He died.
He rose.
He conquered.
He gave.
He saved.
He loved.

We hope.
We try
to overcome.
We too
Would love,
Forgive
As did He.
We fail Him
Often.
Too often.

However
He will
Never fail.
Abba Father,
Jesus Son,
Holy Spirit,
All are One.
As can we
Be One in Him.
Amen.

Tranquility

laughing waters
whisper secrets,
quietly telling
stirring stories,
to captured eddies.

gently soothing
the waterfalls
chuckle, chortle
reflecting all
in mirrored lake.

placid lilies
calmly drifting
upon this lake
God names,
His, Tranquility.

Autumn

Autumn arrives without delay
        And battles for supremacy
        With each, maturing summer day.

Soon rust and amber leaves will fall
        To carpet paths with gentle daubs
        From nature's palette, to enthrall.

The flaming reds with yellows, vie
        To beautify approaching death,
        Thus, we should not fear to die.

Can you hear the spring

Listen!
Hear the sighing of the trees
With their unborn buds of May,
Longing for their cloak of leaves
To herald in the springs birthday?
Hear those whispers through the park?
Feel His presence most profound?
Sense the hope in every heart?
Perceive the stirrings from the ground?
Nature's eagerness, her zeal –
As she stretches out her hand
To direct the spring's caress
Upon her forest and her land.
She breathes, but bides her time –
A pregnant pause – expectancy.
This hush before contraction's push,
readies and helps each shoot to bud,
each precious bulb to bloom,
and every tree, both large and small,
to show their various shades of green.
Nature's birth is God's delight.
So let's take time with Him;
To hear the rustling in the trees,
watch in awe the blossoms bloom.
Come, join us now, its gone so soon!

Summer Daze

Winter's season; a faded utterance.
Spring, maturing, leaves behind her viewpoint.
Summer, breezing in with arrogance –
Warming earth and wisdom's aging joints.

Lazy summer days soon lose their thrill,
No rains to quench, the thirsting rill.
Birds pretend and flutter in scorched earth.
Hydrants burst, inducing child-like mirth.

Sultry dawn, her breakfast, summer's dew,
Green fields turn dun, skies are washed-out blue.
Ceaseless sun gives nature no reprieve
To ease relentless, blaze upon her sleeve.

Breathless prayers entreat for cool respite,
Sweating inner city streets, ignite.
Flies, beleaguer babes, their crying grieves,
Smog-filled skies, inhaled, bring miseries.

Autumn, come, condone no more delay.
Bring your cooling beauty here today!

waiting

All creation's new beginnings.
Wake to stirrings of adoring.
All expecting, waiting, aching.
Stretching up, anticipating,
Beautifying, glorifying,
Giving thanks while testifying.
This new-birth, so purifying,
Sings a song while prophesying.
Hope and life are now reviving
God and earth are harmonizing.

Depression's Gift

low, low my soul,
strained, smeared charcoal-gray,
I scarce can see my
uncontrolled despondency.
depression lays heavy.
i want to scream,
"keep people far away from me,
Lord: overcome my malady."

i no longer care.
weary of being, tired of trying,
mind and body weak, what did i say?
i cannot speak, tongue is tired,
brain is spent, tired, so tired –
just let me be.
so, so weary of this fight.
Listen please! must be alone.

i found myself asleep
upon the office floor
at nine o'clock, this very morn!
I long to find a place to hide.
no people. even those i love.
where can i go?
back to sleeps oblivion?

must find a place of peace
where people will not spout
their pop psychology at me
or give their biblical advice –
making matters worse,
by giving gifts of guilt
thus condemned i feel insane!

am i still your child, O Lord?
have i failed You Father God
failed your Son and Holy Ghost?
i am failure. so confused.
don't know who i am.
all my life i've tried to please.
and my imposter-self
fooled even me.

always performed that
which i thought
'they' expected me to be.
thus, somewhere i lost myself!
i must find the self. where am i Lord?
don't take pills! overcome, overcome!

overcome . . . again?
no! . . . no! . . . no more. i have no strength!
please, please just let me go away!
yet, no one seems to understand.
i have to find myself again!
where can i hide, Lord?
which way? where shall i go?
i wish that i could hibernate.

shame fills my head and skin
making words and thoughts
twist into condemnation.
"try, try harder? trust in Jesus."
Lord, Lord, give me Grace.
soul and spirit fight one another
as the downward force of gravity
draws me toward a murky frightening hole.

i must hold tight. can't let go the rope!
Lord, don't let 'it' pull me down!
the beckoning hole entreats.
the fight to hold becomes too hard.
slowly i slip and slide toward the hole of hell.
"why not let go the rope?" a friend inquires
let go the rope? let go the rope?
i laugh!

let go the rope! of course!

and . . . so i did. no more fight.
heart beats in gratitude.
why did i keep on pulling?
could have let go long ago.
(i wonder if the rope fell down
upon the head of one
who pulled upon the other end?)

"let go the rope."
those simple words, so wise,
showed me that fear and pride
had kept me from the ways of help.
fear of what "they" would think,
pride that i had a need –
"mental health and counseling."
were words of shame for me!

not so now!
the Lord, and they, the helpers,
have given understanding, helping me
to find the me that once was lost
when just a child.
i trust, i know, therefore believe,
that i have found the person
God designed as me!

Sister in Seattle

She sits upon the pavement cold,
Wrapped around in rags of faded hues.
Eyes fixed upon the Latte held in hands to warm
the fingers that thrust through the worn out gloves of blue.
The Latte? Given by a stranger on this freezing Sunday eve.
(An angel or a caring soul? Or – maybe it was you?)
'Could become 10 degrees below tonight.'
booms a passing Dodge car's radio.

She sits beside a bulging plastic bag.
her precious luggage filled with 'objects d'arts'
gathered from her ambles (or her morning jog?)
past the downtown homes that are her Nordstrom stores.
Upon curly steel-gray hair, she wears a cap
(Discarded by a disappointed fan perhaps.)
"Seattle Mariners" it reads "Nineteen Ninety-five."
Regally upon her head, it sits with jaunty pride.
A Queen, decked in her coronation crown!

From sack of paper, brown and stained with fat,
with little finger crooked, she delicately plucks
from within, a "to die for' cinnamon roll,
which she'd found behind the fast food chain
around the corner from her place of rest.
It had beckoned from a bursting garbage can:
these favored gourmet stores for those who live
and sleep and sometimes die upon our streets,
(paved with the gold of Visa, MasterCard,
Discover and American Express!)
'es – 'tis Our Lord's years, two thousand and two, three and four . . . .

Saga of Two Trees

As two trees struggled in life's raging squall,
a flower hid its tiny head from them and wept;
although both growing trees were given strength
by the lashing rains and whirling straws of life;
the buffeting and bruising from the greed
of avarice man's outrageous deeds,
yoked with corruption's fabricated truths;
left these wounded trees alone to bleed –
thus, the flower wept.

The trees, exposed upon the mountainside,
kept in burlap bags, 'til strong enough to plant;
did stand confined, their branches intertwined,
each knowing they must soon release their hold.
Gently, as they weathered each abuse from man,
their branches did they carefully detach
(they had forever had this unity.)

Separated they became –
Liberated, now they swayed in unison;
yet, still close enough to feel the sweet caress
as searching leaves would touch;
for both was proven free and true to love.
Each had their own identity.
Proudly both trees stood sovereign;
The blessed presence of the love divine,
Soothed their fractured hearts, as it surrounded
all the pain of exploitations ways.

Placing all invective's barbs
into the Master-grower's Hand –
He threw the anguish and the pain:
into oblivion's deep.

Now sequestered, but side by side for life,
their Master's tender Hand did plant each tree
upon that bleak and lonely mountain side –
others then would gaze on them in awe;
ponder – how those staunch and steadfast trees
could continue to improve in beauty,
and seem so worshipful?
(Each tree was filled with His Promise
for all those with eyes to see.)

And the flower?
She lifted up her head for she no longer wept;
she had seen the miracle performed upon those trees –
who still endured and suffered; yet, she knew
without a doubt that they would never fail;
but continue to survive and blossom individually –
for each had had the Master's touch for all eternity.

Stars

The stars in the moonlight fascinate me
They seem to be scattered all over the sea,
Twinkling, sparkling, diamonds from welkin,
Buckets of stars, simply, for the taking.
O would I could gather the stars
To sprinkle on those with hurts and with scars,
Making them whole, like some, Robin Hood thief;
I'd distribute the stars to those laden with grief,
And appoint hardened hearts to give hope and relief.

I'd put stars in the eyes of the cold and despised,
Erase hunger's bruise from refugees' eyes.
I'd give away stars in exchange for the guns
And the drugs on the streets that corrupt, little ones.
What joy it would be to be given these ways
To cleanse 'wages of sin' from all yesterdays.
When my bucket was empty, I'd fill it with dreams.
(It's childish illusions with fairy-tale themes.)

However, a Star did come, sparkling with Love
He sprinkled His care with compassion and blood.
This Star touched the sick, the lost and the phony,
Caressed all the mad and the spiritually lonely;
Took away sins from the crib of mankind,
Shielded the righteous, gave sight to the blind.
This Star, the Messiah, Jesus His name,
Gave dreams to fulfill and truths to reclaim.

Stranger

A stranger leaned on the garden gate,
Where a 'sweetheart' lady, with silver hair,
tended her flowers with loving care.
Seeing the stranger, she smiled, a sad smile,
"I'm lonely, you know, though, it has been a while
since my Archie died on a Saturday morning.
It happened so quickly, without any warning!
Won't you come in? I could give you some tea –
but perhaps you've no time to visit with me?"
The stranger said quietly, "I've no other calls!"
"I do miss his laughter, sounds from his footfalls,
which echoed through out these long corridors.
The silence is awful, so empty with gloom.
What would you do with these cold empty rooms?"
"I'd find someone, who had no place to stay;
A pregnant child, or a scared runaway.
I'd look for person who was truly deserving,
A soul, whose existence you'd feel worth preserving.
Your house would then have life in these rooms,
your corridors, echo with footsteps, not gloom.
Their love would embrace your spirit with song –
no longer lonely, your heart would belong."
"No, it would not. What a horrid idea!
My home would be, ransacked. Me – full of fear!
Not only that, what would my friends say?
They'd think I'd gone crazy and stay far away!"
The joy – had she given – to God's needy ones,
The pleasure to Him – if compassion had won.
Both witnessing peoples and angels would stare,
At her Christian love; but, it just wasn't there!
Had she trusted her friends. Showed them the way.
Had she brought to her home just one runaway.
Perhaps, the stranger, may have wanted to share;
He was one of those angels, received unaware!

The Hanging

On death row, a shackled inmate stood
Transfixed by what he saw nailed to the wall.
The warden Al passed by the cell and saw
the convict, riveted with frozen stare.
Al shrugged, snorted, spat and went his way –
eventually to return to apprise
the man, he was to hang at six that day.
The warden walked toward the cell and saw
the man still staring at the empty whitewashed wall.
Al slowed his steps, paused for awhile, then asked –
"Hey you! You there! What are you looking at?"
The inmate shook his head and slowly turned.
His weeping eyes were filled with untold grief,
"Jesus, on that tree. I put Him there!
through anger, violence, drugs and lies.
I'm Barabbas. I should have hung – not Him."
"Don't worry mate, you're going to hang – real soon."
and as the warden walked away, he sneered,
"Christ won't save you now, you bloody fool."
The condemned man grabbed at the jail's cold bars
"Hey! screw wait! Listen! You just don't understand –
I never knew – never saw – His Jesus name.
I played with lust and zeal the devil's game –
I killed the living, damned the dead, but see –
I didn't know, I never saw Him there
Hung naked on the tree for all to watch
His bleeding, thirsting, agonizing pain!
The cross was always empty, with no suffering;
how could I know! He wasn't real – you see?
I'd never seen His shame and agony.
Now I see what he has done upon that tree:
With arms out stretched in love, He set us free –
Damn you screw! HE DIED FOR YOU AND ME!"

With wrenching sobs, before the white-washed wall
    he fell. "Can you forgive me, Lord? – My God,
        I want to be in Paradise with You today!"
    Al turned, cuffed his note and sauntered back
    toward the cell, where open-mouthed he saw
        the man was praying to the empty wall.
Al sighed, shook his head, then softly slipped away
    to fetch the priest – and maybe stopped to pray?

Couple Power

To stride the narrow path as one – each can lead the way.
Foil the devils cunning by not falling by the way.
Couple power is no illusion, its shared autonomy,
A marriage's blessed when one plus one, equals duality.

God's principles are simple. Pray together every day.
Blemish not the wedding ring with desire's depravity.
Unless two walk together, disaster looms ahead.
Alone, one will be tempted from the marriage path and bed.

The highway, broad, will tempt one, with affluence to gain.
That appealing highway's, stewn, with broken vows and pain.
Alone and falling in a ditch of worldly lust and greed
Will bring, a compromising heart to glory, in its shame.

Sometimes in shadows, is the truelove one forsook,
That gleaming ring, now tarnished from its once united look.
Don't opt to walk in solitude and hold the devil's hand.
Repentance and forgiveness can re-shine your wedding band.

Creations Love

(Not a fetus but Creators Life)
Cradled deep within a mothers womb
Begins a tiny seed a being,
A babe, a wonder, a design,
With potential for the future.
Builder, artist, or an author.
A composer, for the people's soul.
Thus begins this breath filled life,
Preordained from worlds beginning
Long before the intercourse of man.
This Holy Gift, blessed for mankind
Develops slowly. Features form.
Fragile personality is wrought.
Then tender as a butterfly kiss,
A tiny beat, confirms the Life within.

Hands

Hands are for working,
for loving, for giving,
for playing, for mending
the sick.
Hands can be shocking,
be gentle, be pretty,
be perfect, be strong,
or be weak.
Hands can be willing
to toil for each other,
to offer, to tender,
and care.
Hands can tell stories
of hardship, of sorrow,
of beauty, of aging,
of prayer.

Hope

some wander through the wilderness of life
without a star to navigate the way,
or a friend who's qualified to guide.
thus they meander, lonely, empty and bereaved.
some live a life of self-deceptive peace,
which glorifies the enemy of man.
'tis hopelessness and intellectual pride
this tranquil poultice to a soul that yearns
unknowingly, for God's, respect and love.
life's perfect, peaceful, masterpiece.
darkened angels, lock with mirth, heaven's gates,
while lucifer? he grins and rubs his hands in glee!
Gods' way is crystalline,
not muddied with some phantom words.
the verity, my friends, is here;
Jesus Christ, died for the world, that all,
should have eternal life and love,
perpetually.

Once there was sweet Motherhood

Sacrifice of self; seems no more.
Womanhood now demands its privilege
"It's my body, I have my human rights."
Does wee one have no civil liberties?
Must baby sacrifice its life, its future,
Because of sexual appetite?
"I love you Mama! I am here,
Mama can't you feel my fear?"
Hardened hearts no longer feel.
Loves grown cold,
So sorry precious little one,
You seem to have no rights at all,
So simply sacrifice your life.
You're just a consequence of sin,
Maybe from rape or passions fling.
Yours is a martyr's death for another's sin.
I hear a cry. "Crucify Him."

the perfect friend

they hear with eyes intent on what i say.
eyes stay fixed and do not flitter,
side to side, or wander far away.
the tilt of head, encouraging,
and with their gentle smile,
i feel special, confident to speak.
soon,
i discern that something, is unique;
inhibited i falter, words then swiftly fade;
for this rapt listener is rare.
no interruption do they make.
they are not compelled to have
their say.
when we part, a warmth surrounds --
self-worth is strong, i strive no more;
at least no more today.

Dedicated to Darlene Cunningham, a true friend to so many and to me.

The Promise

Through Winter's coat, sun-rays bugle
As nature murmurs to her bowers
Warming her earth with snowy mantle
While waking snowdrops, Winter's flower.
Each crystal morning offers peace,
Bringing hope to Springs' elation
To those who see God's masterpiece
And extol with veneration.

Cold birds puffed up, in Winter's pride,
Feathered breasts daubed blushing-red.
Snowflakes cascade on Spring's new bride,
Luxuriant white her featherbed.
Squirrels sprint and prink and probe,
Hidden berries, prized caché.
Cloaked holly trees in bright wardrobe
Help dress the earth in her display.

Jeweled streams astound in velvet night,
While moonbeams sequin naked trees.
Formed icicles, chilled stalactite,
Softly chime their allegory
Of hope for man's eternal climb.
This Winter's tale corroborates
With those that wait and take the time
To praise, revere and contemplate.

True Gain

It would profit nothing;
should one's body burn,
in Martyrdom, and one not love.
Clearly, these words state that
loveless sacrifice is death.
Do not the words request compassion,
without compromise?
The Word with us in partnership,
while suffering a cup to sip,
does say – to pray, to go, to give.
Yet, oneself will gain pure joy,
as true love meets the untold pain
of hurting peoples –
To care, to love, to weep,
with those who weep, brings joy untold,
with peace, that passes every
understanding given man.

Unconditional Forgiveness

Forgiveness is no more a choice in this age of famine,
Bloody wars, divorce, denial and racial bigotry.
If you can win the wrestle, that hard wrestle to forgive,
Peace will tenure in its place, swallowing the negative!

We must forgive the misery – the memory of abuse,
The trauma suffered as a child – those hurts we hold so close.
Forgive injustice and the pain of being second-best,
The wounding of that hurtful word a parent said in jest.

"Forgive? You know not what you say! Forgive? It's not deserved.
Forgive! No way! More like their head upon a platter served."
No one can know the pain or the injustice done, it's true.
But to be free you must forgive, so Christ will forgive you too.

Stored sin becomes as cancer, inflaming sores that seep,
Self-pities steeped in matted sins that fester as they sleep.
Sins of bitterness encrust one's inner soul with weeping.
Self-pity loves itself so much, it cannot be forgiving!

One's collected sins accept, though another was the cause.
The Forgiver will forgive if you repent and love His laws.
Look closely in a mirror. View your reflected self.
Look face-to-face and eye-to-eye. Now . . . forgive yourself.

Once done you'll find it easier, those persons to absolve,
They who abused, defiled, tormented, mind and soul.
When you have won the battle you'll feel clean and purified,
Dear friend, by "the forgiving wrestle" you'll be sanctified.

With peace of mind new joy of life, depression soon will wane!
You'll not forget but the forgiving will annihilate the pain.
From your deep-seated un-forgiveness, He's forgiven you –
And freedom is His Gift, when you forgive as He has you.

A Tear

And there He hung
Before the multitude
Offering His Life,
His Heart and Soul,
His Love for the whole world
In worship to His Father;
However, did those prying eyes
understand
The single tear He shed,
Was grief for them?

Capriciousness

Foxes had holes, and birds had their nest;
But Christ was grateful wherever He'd rest.
This was, quite often, some grassy knoll bed
With no pillow to rest His weary head.
Tranquility's peace would always be His,
In spite of the burden and endless needs,
From confused people, the lost, and diseased.
He baptized, comforted, taught and He healed
He'd listen to all; man, woman and child.
Cries for forgiveness, entreated requests,
For His healing, His touch and later . . .
His death.

Early Prayer

Each dew drenched morning, early
a solitary man arose
to the music of the dawning.
Cool amid hazy were those first lights,
when I'd see his lonely figure,
striding forth, with joyous steps,
toward a misty mountain place
to pray and seek his Father's Face,
upon that waiting mountainside.

Once there, He'd find a spot to kneel
then pray unto His Abba God.

All too soon, like sheep, the mob,
(disciples, too!) would find Him gone,
and so would scurry hurriedly
to find, the praying man, they loved,
and by so doing, they'd disturb
His precious time, alone with God.
I thought I heard Him whisper there
as the crowds were drawing, near,
"Not My will but Yours I'll bear."

How did He pray?
What were His prayers?
Petition for His Spirit's rest,
or for His soul to be refreshed;
from early man's polluted best?
What did His Heavenly Father share?
Divine instructions for the day??
What did He ask?
The answer, friend, I cannot tell -
I'm Mary, and they're personal!

From Hills of Joy

As early morning dew glistens
And jewels of Heaven shine
May I too shine for You Lord.
Bringing Joy unto Your Heart
Laughter to your Spirit.

Take from me all wicked ways
Evil thought and attitudes
Preserve my soul for You.
That I may dwell and sing
In Your Presence ever more.

Come hearts melody and sing
With gratitude to Him
Who is patient, kind, and true
This Creator of all that was,
That is, and still to come.

Sing my soul and spirit sing
Songs of praise and glory
Unto Him the Father King
Let us tell His awesome story
From the Hills of Joy within.

How long?

how long should He care?
how long must He weep?

outwardly no stain of tear.
however, from within, a weeping,
battered, bruised and beating heart,
still throbs, with unconditional love.

this loving heart?

it weeps for ignorance,
as evil's subtlety persists.
'tis bruised
because of man's deceptive ways.
'tis battered
by our endless hopelessness –
yet His heart, still throbs
for our eternity,
as we, by ourselves, still
try to endure.

perhaps there is still time to learn,
and from our sad predicaments return,
to sow and reap, some better seed
to gladden God's own heart
with hope for us again.

how long should He care?
how long must He weep?

until . . .?

Jesus Was His Name

Jesus was His name
From the Creator, God He came
Came as a babe – a lowly babe
Born of a virgin, it is said.
He was a King – a Royal King
Whose Kingdom was not yet to be
Until his subjects, one and all,
Could truly love their enemy.
Jesus was His name –
Who washed sin, dust, and grime,
From off men's feet, so many times.
He laughed and sang with fisherman.
He was their loyal and faithful friend,
A mentor from despair for them.
He gave Himself to serve and save
The soul of man from out the grave.
He chose to die a convict's death.
Hung crucified upon a tree
He died with joy within His heart.
He knew His death would set men free.
And those who serve Him willingly
He shall always love and cherish,
For He died for you and me.
Therefore, through sin we will not perish.
Jesus is His name
From the Creator – God He came.

Substance in Shadow

Shadows are different, they seldom are warm,
Some are quite chilly, unpleasant, forlorn.
Especially when shadows come from the fame,
Of one who is known, to the public by name.
Fixed quietly in shadow, obscure and unknown,
As a solitary substance, I stand there, alone.
My festering feelings, ranted and raved.
Ugly thoughts surged toward those who rejected.
At the rudeness, ill manners, and lack of urbanity.
Anger and pain, caused my substance to seethe.
(Rejection eclipses all love with such ease.)

My love in the limelight, always, knew
Of my anger and pain from within his shadow.
I majored on insults and slights 'till the day
When I saw a figure, just a whisper away.
He was vaguely familiar to me . . . in a way
Could it be? Was it? The Lord in the shade?
After all of the sacrifices that He had made.
No one, but He, ever had such rejection,
Yet, He forgave and loved all with compassion.
Even today, He's continually spurned
I must confess shame, for now that I see
He is the Substance in Shadow . . . not me.

The Man of Sorrow

A lonely man,
Surrounded by the twelve.
A Holy man,
Always giving of Himself.
A grieving man,
Healing the sick,
A Loving man,
Who died on Calvary.

This Love

As a gentle tide, soothing, calm.
Serenity caresses me
'Tis equal to a gentle kiss
Saturating mind and spirit.
Giving repose to yearning souls,
With tranquility and peace.
This –
Is His everlasting love.

Warmth of love

Let not my love grow cold.
Tie it to your waist Lord.
Stay the flow
of Your Broken Heart
For it is the warmth
Of Love that keeps
Me deep within Your Grace

Who

how many leaves upon a tree
or petals in a bride's bouquet?
how many stars hang in the sky,
or grains of sand on oceans lay?
who can count them? who would try
to capture twinkles from an eye,
or a baby's smile retain?
could you do it? nor could I.

but I know of One on high who
collects each tear that's shed –
One who knows when sparrows die,
and every hair upon your head –
One who cares to give and love,
who weeps when you are hurting –
One who longs to take your pain
and give life everlasting.

Easter Day

The human smell of excrement and sweat.
Raucous amusement from screaming multitudes.
"Death to the impostor! Crucify, Crucify"
Violence desecrates this soon Holy Day.
"Is This your King, King of the Jews"
Sarcastic, sneering words echoed
Through the Streets of Dolorosa.
"How weak and pitiful he is, NOT dignified!
Someone help him with his cross. Come on!
Or he won't make it up the hill and thus be crucified.
Hey You there! You black barbarian
lend a hand for this 'royal majesty'", he mocked.

At first afraid, bewildered and alarmed
by the hate and noise of Romans, Jews alike.
The battered, bleeding man was gently helped
by the Cyrene and the lifting of the cross,
from the bloodied broken back and weeping knees,
"Why are you, King, so badly used?" he murmurs to the man
"With whips, derisions. Why are you mistreated so?"
The man looked into the Cyrene's eyes with gentle smile,
He whispered, "Be you not afraid dear Simon.
Simply believe I am your King, Messiah, the promised One.
I will not forget you, good and faithful friend
And one day soon you will understand."

Good Friday

How His Mother, Mary suffered,
His friends, each martyred
Yet, where is compassion now
for Mary's Precious Son?
His Father suffered deeply too
For He knew what was to come
To this Savior of mankind
Jesus Christ, His Only Son.
How can we fully understand?
God's agony and breaking heart
As He turned and left His Son
Alone to bear the hammered Pain.
Pain! From thirst and brutal nails
Pain! Where had His Father gone?
Pain! From a Breaking Heart,
Pain! Wondering if we'd believe
His sacrifice had given liberty.
Gave us our Father God once more
So we could bond with Him again
Forgiven and for all Eternity.
Forgive us Lord our lack
Of gratitude. Our selfishness.
Our deafened ears, and eyes so blind
To Your Holy Sacrificial Lamb.
Yet His Loving Heart still overflows,
His sacrifice, is limitless.
His Love so pure, unwarranted,
Cascades forth, yet is unrequited still.
Abba Father, forgive us once again,
Help our Soul and Spirit to entwine,
In Holiness and thus prevail to win the race
So we may spend Eternity with Him in You.

Jerusalem

Jerusalem: City where the Prophets died
a martyr's death, at frightened unbelieving hands.
The prophets' sin? They spoke God's message without fear.
And you thought you were doing God a favor. So
you killed to drown the words that rang within your ear.

Jerusalem: City of the Lord Christ Jesus.
The Rose of Sharon, wandered through your cobbled street.
Spoke in your Temple, as a boy of twelve. Forthright –
words of grace and wisdom fell from His youthful lips,
amazing learned priests, who listened to His Scripts.

Jerusalem (City that your Holy God still loves.)
Where the Lily of the Valley, was betrayed
in the Garden of Gethsemane, while He prayed!
This Man, just thirty-three, the Virgin Mary's heir,
was crucified beside your busy thoroughfare.

Jerusalem: City of the Holy Spirit.
Pilgrims come to "walk-the-walk" your Messiah took,
up the Via Dolorosa; the street, with tortured breath.
On this cobbled street, where His followers come to pray;
People shriek their wares, where once they screamed 'Crucify'

Jerusalem: City of Christ crucified.
Commercialism spreads its curse from church to church.
On 'Holy sites' where once He preached, they claim!
Selling, hawking, peddling icons, baubles, trinkets –
Still, you dishonor Fathers' House with mammon's shame!

Jerusalem: City over which He wept.
'Twas thus, because He saw, that through the present,
past and future, you learned, zilch, as years have fled.
You're still a tree without a fig to serve your Lord.
"Peace, you cry. We've suffered much."
                    True, and so has He.

once upon a tree

and so,
it came to pass;
at last
at thirty-three,
upon a tree
he died
for you
and me.
which gives us life
if we believe;
for all eternity.

Potentate

With breathless joy, a babe, a boy,
a son, to early manhood grew,
to rule, and reign for all eternity.
No earthly king but carpenter –
(which still confounds humanity!)
The world had waited long
for this Savior's awesome love,
yet, when it saw the depth of it,
it scoffed at him and laughed
as He hung dying on a tree.
This Love: has waited centuries
for people, country, nations,
to accept this healing Jew.
He was God's awaited promise.
A strong and gentle leader,
deliverer, potentate was He.
Most people still ostracize
His gift of liberty, from sin
so death would have no longer sting.
His portrayal of selfless Love
(of which most, are still suspicious.)
have people wonder. "Can this be true?
Dare we believe?" they ask.
"Was He the promised one?
Was His sacrificial love for me?
Can He really take away my sin
that I may have eternity?
Will He forgive?"
I know He has no favorites.
He envelops all with love.
Jew, Greek, Asian, sinners all.
He died that the whole world
from sin, would be relieved,
if only we believe, we would be free,
forgiven, and receive.

The Vase

Close beside a wooden cross, stood a vase upon a shelf;
A chronicled alliance – God creations – symbolized.
The alabaster urn, a Virgin vase of beauty,
created to encompass and to ever love her Rose.
She tenderly enfolded
this bloom of love within her;
her perfumed prayers ascending
gave pleasure to the Father.

She was of rare design, this protector of the Rose,
a Vase created milky white, in alabaster prose.
Not by clay or plaster was she molded by the Potter;
No fissure or blemish was in the Vase to spoil her.
This maiden was created,
a jewel of opal beauty,
to protect and to cherish
God's own Son, the Sharon Rose.

This figurine of loveliness, pondered in her heart,
With knowledge in her spirit, from life He'd soon depart –
Silent was her weeping as sorrow pierced her breast.
Her Rose would soon be sacrificed for humanity's bequest.
Against her will she lingered,
watching as each petal fell;
drops of blood upon the earth
to depose the king of hell.

He cried "Father! forgive them, for they know not what they do."
Such profound forgiveness, amazed all beside His cross.
Then sky grew dark with misery, while raining tears of woe.
Yet, the Vase was strangely comforted, standing there below
For she heard His whispered Words,
"My Dear Woman, here's your son."
To John "Here is your Mother."
To His Father, "It is done!"

Georgia Straits

Moody and deceptive,
Flow the seas of Georgia Straits.
Today, the sea is flat and gray
Reflecting washed out sun.
It's peaceful, as the moment,
The sea appears quite calm.
Yet, the wily wind can kick-up
Like a stalking predator,
Crouched, carefully waiting,
like a wild beast for his kill.
The unsuspecting prey of course,
The lone sailor with his skill.

Glacier Bay

Blanket fog muffled sound.
Thick and cold. Suffocating.
Cheating eye and ear
As my love and I sail silently,
Each eye straining to pierce the shroud
Which hung beneath the unseen sky.
Graveyard silence, smothering
In it's leaden-gray intensity.

Abruptly Nature's curtain rose,
Startled, stupefied and stunned were we
By the sight which was revealed.
A glorious scene appeared before our eyes.
Awesome was the shock of sudden beauty
From those majestic, snow-capped mountains,
Crowned with halos' from a golden sun.

It was as though we came from death to life –
From darkness into radiant Light.
An internal prayer of gratitude
Arose for our wondrous gift of sight.
All that day our soaring spirits sang
With dulcet music flowing through our hearts
To Him;
from whom this special day had come.

Harvest Moon

Dappled cloud, pinkish gray, dress the afternoon's dull day.
Breathlessly the sun arrives, peeking shyly through the gray.
"Much too late to warm the day," seems to say a tender doe.
"The day," mimics, from Madrona tree, a raven black.
An eagle soaring, salmon dinner in her clutch - agrees.
We too accede, as we navigate the Inland Passage way.
These untamed scenes delight the eye as we sail
to find a sheltered anchorage, in which to end our day.
Palely glows the Moon - time for God to light His gloaming skie
and caress, the velvet night with His galaxy of stars;
which chaperon and guide loan sailors with His moonlit paths.
Beneath this canopy of God's - safely anchored - we give thanks
To Him, in awe and gratitude for beauteous nights like this.

Magical Morning

Magical Morning! His mirrored Creation.
Mists apparition, give a heart liberation.
Eagles, stand sentry, on solemn old timber.
Fish make mouth-whirlpools,
their silver scale shimmer.
No one is near, to bring pain and alarm;
Only a bee humming nature's new psalm.
This magical morning's effervescent bequest?
Nothing more than a man's spirit refreshed.

Morning Glory

Silver-gray dawning.
Peeps from a nestling.
Enthralling quiet,
soothes, through the dawn.
Silence; its softness,
fills this rare morning.
Time, seems to stand still,
in tranquilities peace,
Calm is my spirit
drinking in dews cologne.
Sun kindly probes
morning mist with her light;
as nature's serenity;
comforts my soul.

The Artist

a rare and gentle painter,
with his palette, and his brushes;
tints, with early morning tones,
brushing mystery with mist.
His skill, touches all creation,
pledges hope, with rainbow oath.
He finishes with zealous stroke,
painting tranquility, with truth.
varnishing with aurora's glow,
glazing skillfully the fragile light.
the image, on his canvas,
mixed with mystic form?
the beauty of the birthing
of His glorious new dawn.

A Prayer

Lord Jesus,
Come and see
If my Soul,
My Spirit,
All my Heart
And Strength
Belong to Thee.
If they do not
Forgive me,
Please!
Deliver me
From me
That I can wholly
Worship Thee.
And my deep love
You'll plainly see.
Amen

End Times

Day breaks anxiously, tinged phantom gray,
as smoldering clouds of Armageddon, brew.
Whitecaps no longer chaste with foaming spume,
for oceans' tumbling waves are horsed with debris
as they pound the shores of our ancestors land
with scum and evidence of human waste;
while oiled sea-creatures, sing a deathwatch hymn.

Birds, caked in slime, no longer gently glide
and skim the glittering sea for teeming fish
that once did sport beneath this spoil of man.
The sun no longer shimmers from blue sky.
Acrid pollution veils this orb of God;
blood red it glows, an eye infected by
the virus from pollution's malady.

Heat upon the day, scorches precious land,
Cold saturated nights, chill the heart of man.
Power games, human wars of greed. A dearth
of God's love for our neighbor as ourselves.
Beloved world, which had in isolation dreamed;
now aches beneath the wrath of God's disease,
and science gamely battles 'gainst mans plight.

'Tis no matter, man will soon a vapor be,
we are destroyed; whom can we blame?
Global warming, terrorism, still take us by surprise.
Dead fish, warm seas, and we wonder why?
The human race has ravaged life, however
if we try – maybe, there's time to change;
giving man a glimpse of God again.

Eternity

Heart, Spirit, Soul,
Plus flesh makes life.
Heart dies – eventually,
Soul and spirit, wend their way
Toward the Creator's Light.
His beckoning Love
And Truth will shine,
Dazzling Heaven's radiance,
Guiding each souls final flight
Toward Him, who awaits to say,
"Well done, my friend,
You are so welcome here today!"
Thus, eternity begins!

charity?

few people grieve for the human race
that soon may be extinct;
through lack of love
lack of heart
lack of empathy.
many fight for whale,
gorilla, spotted owl
or dying redwood tree;
Has this become misguided,
an erroneous charity
that brings about a heinous cost –
if balanced not, with equal care,
with precious human dignity?

darkness

once upon a time the shadows came.
the wings of velvet nights did gently fall,
encompassing the earth with cloak of warmth.
no fear was known, just comfort in each home.
the cloak gave its security to all –
peace overflowed, and this was meant to be.

now – anger, sickness, mayhem, stalk the night.
fear breeds and multiplies itself.
the warriors of hate – corruption's saints –
curse love and pity. Hate's their opiate.
the devil's hoards, human in their cunning,
deftly riffling pure and gentle souls.

hearts beat in time with fear which stalk the nights,
whispered prayers are prayed in fervid hope.
the warring games of greed and death proceed –
plundering with rage, raping, earth and sky;
fumes are released from hell, to suffocate
the virtuous ones – yes Armageddon's nigh!

Desperate Dignity

Flotsam, from the spiral of depression,
accumulates upon the tide of life.
The jobless, black and white, search for work,
expecting livelihood for pride again.
Slowly, celebrating hearts, filled with hope,
turn to mourning, as time and time they hear:
"We're sorry folks, we have no work for you."
"The shelters?" "Full, I'm afraid! No room!"
No work, no room (No stable at the inn?)
Still believing, hoping for employment,
many wait with child-like faith, trusting prayers
may help, to light a spark of human care
and give them work to salvage dignity.
How long must human suffering cling
to its worry raft of desperation?
Beneath a bridge many still convene:
for hope deferred will make the hearts of those
who linger for desired reprieve, unwell.
Depression turns to thoughts of suicide,
discouragement, drives some to reckless drink,
while tarrying wives and children left behind
in destitution's throe, wait hopefully
for news that soon, they once again will eat.
Can no one hear the children cry?
Does anybody care the needy must return
with empty hopes, their mission failed once more?
Does God have children, are they deaf or dead?
Meanwhile –
victim's wane until they become
a compost heap of broken hearts and debts.

False Appearance

Silence, peace, tranquility –
No sound of man or limousine.
No breath of future machination.
A whispered cloud, soft vapor,
lazily drifts through azure sky:
but beneath – a shadow, dark and cold,
stalks the unsuspecting earth.

Actuality confronts, while
weeping nature, prophesies the truth.
Why is actuality never seen?
Is it because, man, prefers delusion's shield
with fabricated dreams – not verity?
The imprudent cannot see.
They are blinded by false hopes that shine,
and thus, effluvium fades away!

Beware, all peoples. Darkness steals,
and gives false peace, and thus achieves,
the worst; one government, one church.
Worshipers: be prepared for razed illusions;
for the unseen specter, ever stalks.

Sweet Brother

My dear, dear brother
wait not too long with
intellect superior.
listen to the Word
that has no end -
making men, far
wiser men than you,
bend to its ways.
O sightless eyes
so arrogant and blue -
attracted by the world.
O deafened ears
that hears the babble -
loves the loudness
of boom-box steel,
experiments with drugs and alcohol.
All too soon, soiled morals,
ethics, social laws,
become a ravished,
raped and broken life.

War Games

Drop by drop from Ancient days; the blood of youth has rained
Upon the earth, both here and faraway in distant lands.
The young blood permeates through many nations' mood
As youth of both the victors and the vanquished spilled their
blood
For love of family, and country, with freedom as their core,
However, did their dying justify the end? Is was no more?

When victory has been won, does everybody then suppose,
That all is well – because war is done and peace has been
declared?
Do not those cries for mothers, still on winds abide?
Did not, do not, both enemy and victor's bodies lay
In Flanders Field, in jungles, broken cities, side by side,
Together, decomposing in some unmarked foreign grave?

Does not each warring country suffer mortal loss of life?
Are returning heroes, untouched by death, they smelled or saw?
Veteran addicts were conceived, given birth and weaned on drugs,
because of fear, fatigue, humid heat and sucking bugs.
The crippled, maimed through some brave deed or rescue of a pal,
Or sniper bullet, unseen mine or tortures' unknown hell.

The disturbed, the battle scarred (the wounded brain)
Violence is now protection to relieve internal pain.
The sightless, blinded by explosions in the line of fire –
Let us not forget those blinded by a memory
Of some performed atrocity, committed by decree
Given from behind the lines by eager military.

They were denied, defiled, betrayed by rash cupidity
Which glorifies the sin of man's profane depravity.
The Pharisees of long ago – they still walk, my friends:
Hypocrites, who with subtle theft, stalk their prey with praise,
Power play, pride-filled disdain, and finally corruption.
How can we right wars' wrongs and prohibit its resumption?

All peoples young and old with aching hearts and empty arms
Must weep with wrenching suffering at war's futility.
War starts because of parsimonious men, their lust for dignity,
Power to rule, to conquer those who had to fight for liberty –
Enticing youth to war, to kill and mutilate through lies
Our youth, perverted by the devil's tool, of compromise!

The Crying Earth

Victory's a fallacy, a lie and hoax.
A mirage, in the distant sands of time.
Why do we justify the wars, the hangings, murders of a babe?
"I have my right," is everybody's cry.
Must babes also be sacrificed, to satiate the thirst for self?
Reprisals that will corrupt the soul of human race,
The cries for blood, a growing grave for all society.

I should proclaim repentance, to turn this war-like craze
That penetrate most media, our streets and homes these days.
'Forgive me Lord; Forgive,' should be my battle cry!
Can I not bury differences and pray for God's supply
Of forgiveness, truth and love, and care for others more.
Before further blood is sacrificed upon this earth through war?

One prayer will make the difference if it's meant with all my heart
If I just practice what I preach then this will be the start.
If I don't pray and precious blood of babes, is spilled again
I'll be in part responsible for useless deaths and pain,
For none shall be exempt from – disgrace and staining shams,
As blood from generations, meet the Sacrificial Lamb's.

Cancer's Pain

One, Two. One-Two-Three.
Count the pauses after pain.
Four-Five. Four, Five, Six.
Pulse races with fear.
One, Two. Three-Four-Five.
Fear of what? Soon be free!
Six-Seven. Seven-Eight-Nine.
Fear of leaving family.
Lord, cherish them. Six-Seven.
Go pain! Go away!
There is no victory –
Death had no sting for me.
For I believe. Two-Three.
I have eternal life. Four-Five
I am coming Lord, six-seven. eight …

grand-mama

She stirs.
eyes move beneath the veil of age.
She sighs.
a moan, as eyelids thinly veined
are gently forced by nature's light
to open to another day.
"O Lord!"
A sleepy prayer, a whispered plea
from aged, parched and pallid lips?
some agitated memory,
a souvenir of yesterday –
filter through her clearing mind,
as slumber fades, then drifts toward
the cold reality of day.
Languid realization slowly dawns;
"O no!
No family today. No joy."
Too soon, it will begin again,
those endless hours stretched before,
old memories' lone company,
arthritic pain, an enemy
who waits impatiently to wean
Great Grand-mama
from Halcion's medicated dream.

Mardi

Saying farewell we saw her time was near;
She knew us not, but gave a wistful smile.
She passed away upon a perfect day
of breaching whales and mirrored sea.
Blood-red sunset, glorifying God,
Angel-wing-like clouds punctuating love.
Sorrow, joy mixed both our hearts with grief
though tears did stain our cheeks, there was relief.
For she was, free, at last, from pain and stress,
She'd waited long to take her journey home
and know
His peace
His Truth
His Way
His Life.
And we can thus believe the angels sang,
and trees and flowers, such as we have never seen
joined in with praises for this weary one,
as upon the emerald meadows' green
her Savior welcomed her – with open arms
and said, "Well done! Well done!"

A Baby Cries

Hush! A baby cries: come weep with me!

The world awaits: in stillness it anticipates
A regal King, a glamorous Lord – but stay!
What is that you say?
A Servant filled with Love and Charity
Has already come and died for me.
The Christ? How ridiculous!
He was too bleak and strangely ugly.

His intensity over-powered those he knew.
No, no. Too stark. He had no regal dignity.
A Majesty, a King with Glory,
Was the expectation for our world
Which, by the way, has waited and still waits,
For a Savior, from Heaven, a Lord.

Look here – if as you say, He was this love incarnate,
Why did He appear completely void
Of ancient custom, ritual and liturgy?
Some say that He was barren of all selfishness,
Of sentiment and compromise.
If He was the Son of God,
Why did He not conform
To God's Holy Sabbaths ways?

No, no! He was too strong. Too radical.
He did not tolerate those merchants in the temple!
Make the lame to walk, the blind to see!
They said He was Beelzebub!
What's that you say?
". . . a house divided cannot stand!"

Too clever with His words.
Oh yes! He seemed gentle in His strength.
His love? A different love of selfless love.
Which had not been seen before or since.
Pray tell, how could this man be He,
Whom we have long awaited through years of war,
Decades of fear, pogroms and holocaust?

If He was the promise from above,
The promise to a Nation, shattered,
Scattered far and wide.
Moreover, I am not saying that He is –
Then – I agree,
He was born two thousand years ago.
Is the Way, the Truth, the Life

Was a man. Was Mary's infant Son.
Was crucified upon a tree
Was the Sacrificial Lamb,
The Christ. Messiah. Great High Priest.
The only Son of God.
So tell me why is He still
Rejected in His guise as man?

My ears don't hear. My eyes don't see.
My heart it does not understand

Hush! A Baby cries; come weep with me!

Pilgrims

All too soon, we find we are September,
in the autumn of our earthly years.
We recall achievements and remember;
the hopes and doubts that molded our careers.
We muse and wonder, what has happened to those years
that fled through life with laughter and with tears?
We had struggled hard to find out who we were.
Now we know, of course, we no longer care.
Why did it take so long?
Does wisdom come too late at evensong?
No!
Each must travel forward, on life's cane,
Though every step may bring distressful pain.
Ever advancing pilgrims should progress,
like émigrés, must walk and not digress.
Onward, onward, day by day toward
the finish line; to win ones life's reward,
and hear, one hopes, the acclamation
from our Friend,
for a mammoth race, well hobbled to the end.

Celebrations

Christmas celebrations: what are the reasons? Why?
The answer has been written down, a gentle lullaby,
A soothing song of living words that birthed this giving time.
A time of carols, groaning boards and presents to entwine.
From church bells sweet, a melody, divine nativity,
Bring memories of Bethlehem and gifts of prophecy.

First gold, a yellow metal, glows bright for preciousness,
Then frankincense, rare fragrance pure, to burn for sacrifice,
And myrrh, a sweet anointing oil for God's ordained high priest.
These special gifts were given by the Magi from the east
To celebrate the Virgin birth of Christ the infant king,
To prophesy salvation through his future suffering.

Christ Jesus was the title given this Holy Sovereignty
Born within a stable bare, no pomp or majesty.
The promise of the Father came as just a lowly child
Born from the womb of Mary, blest Virgin, not beguiled.
Babe wrapped in love, tied with grace, destined to forgive
Both you and me, when He was nailed so crudely on that tree.

So let's not forget the reason, the reason for it all,
The Christmas celebration and the decking of the hall.
Let's not forget God's chosen gift was spiked upon a tree,
As joyously, we trim our tree in its festivity.
Let's not forget that Christmas is much more than gifts and fun;
Remember, it's the Birthday of Christ Jesus, God's own Son!

Peace Shall Come Again

Peace shall come again,
however not before –
dark clouds and thunderous skies
with fearful blast, divide and scroll;
as swiftly on the wings of wind, Abba Father,
God, Jehovah, Yahweh, our Creator,
Frightful, Awesome in His Love and Justice,
Rides once more, with chariot ablaze and sword before.
Then – the final trump shall sound its story
Heralding the Prince of Peace in Glory.
The Sacrificial Lamb, The Christ, Messiah,
Holy King, Beloved Son of Righteousness.
Where upon, each weeping woman, man and child
whatever color, culture, race or creed,
shall kneel, bow, and in their tongues, concede
the Savior, Great Messiah, Christ the King,
has come, to reign, in all His Majesty.
Then – ultimately – in wondrous unity,
shall Hosannas ring and Hallelujahs rise
As Jesus, gives the everlasting prize –
To those of His who ran the race to win
The right to live, eternally, with Him.
Yes! Then – peace shall come again.

The Nativity

A snowflake. Night both crisp and clear.
Sequined heaven's velvet curtain
Rose, and the future was revealed;
Bringing forth an awed applause,
From all creation waiting there.

A super star threaded through the Milky Way –
A glorious dazzling star so bright
It all but blinded for a moment those that say,
"Twas as a lantern in the Hand of God that night."
Shepherds buried heads in arms and prayed.

Silently the star shined forth while angels sang,
Then moved toward a town, named Bethlehem.
The few who followed it, were led toward
A crib, a manger bed, within a stable's care.
Shepherds, Magi, gathered at the door.

They stood; then overcome,
They knelt in awe upon the straw
As cattle lowed, breathed their warmth,
Upon the nestled family there
Among the straw and bales of hay.

Therefore, a destined, fated life began
Among the chosen few that worshipped
At this tiny infant's feet. This babe?
The once and future King, who smiled;
While angels sang their joyous lullaby.

Which art in heaven

Almighty God, Abba, Father,
Yahweh, Fortress, Judge.
The I AM, of all Creation;
Heaven, Living Things,
Earth, Sea and Springs,
Woman, Child and Man.

The Son of God: His Names –
The Christ, Messiah, Lord,
Savior of the chosen few,
The Risen, He stands true
Jesus, Spirit, Prophet,
Testimony of Trinity.

Earthquakes, Famine, War.
Warnings – Armageddon's near.
Holy sickles, sharpened.
Fury, Wrath of God,
Justice rides upon White horse,
Eyes ablaze with Righteousness.

Devil, Destroyer, Demon-god,
False Prophet, Beast, Beelzebub,
Apollyon, Mephistopheles,
Deceiver of all Nations.
Ancient Serpent, Bound,
Hurled, locked and sealed in Abyss
For a thousand years to hiss.

Satan freed, on bond,
Deceives Nations. Gathers Marchers
Into war and . . . loses!
Eventually to burn in Sulfer Lake made for
the wicked falled ones.

Saints chorus, Angels sing.
Elders fall at Holy Feet,
Worship with a song of Praise.
Marriage, Banquet, Feast –
Christ Bride Joins her Groom,
All Heaven Celebrates.

O Bright and Glorious Morning Star –
King Eternal, Great High Priest,
The Way, the Truth, the Life.
Prince of Peace, Rising Sun, Bread of Life,
The Christ, Messiah, Everlasting Father!
Come Soon Dear Lord. Come Soon!
It is enough!

the perfect gift

There is a gift more precious
than silver, gold entwined.
A gift of joy that is adorned,
with fondness, grace combined.

The needy heart with faith
esteems this gift divine,
laced with worth, bound with love,
tied and bowed in kind.

Wrapped in trust and confidence,
security anointed,
This precious gift, unheralded,
taken so for granted.

This gift of so much worth?
This treasure to preserve?
A friend! A friend in every way,
A friend so undeserved.

We remember, Father,
your Son, who called us "friend,"
a friend who gave His very life,
that ours should have no end.

Thank you, God, for friends,
dear ones, both old and new.
They are a gift to treasure;
such friends may we be too!

New Years Resolution

With persistence a lone leaf clings.
To an old trees naked bough
I seem to be clinging too
To every past years painful slough.

Why can't I forgive and release
All the anger inside and the blame.
A Resolution I'll make now to cease.
And to never look backward again.

As that lone leaf finally falls
And yields to the New Years call
I cleave to Hopes new Peace
Allowing Joy to replace my release.

I will yield my cloak of self pity
And dress in the robe of Grace
I will scorn and release all anguish
So forgiveness can take its place.

Let Joy replace all our releases
Leave them entombed in the past
Never look backward just forward
Give Thanks for His Love that lasts.

Index